he *Magical* TASTE of SUMMER GRILLING

Chef/Stylist: Cole Croghan
Photography: Guy Rogers

the *Magical* TASTE of SUMMER GRILLING

1720 Regal Row, Suite 112, Dallas Texas. 75235.
Phone: 214.630.4300.

ISBN: 1-879234-63-7

Publisher: Rodney L. Dockery

Editorial Director: Caleb Pirtle III
Project Manager: Robyn Rogers
Food Editor/Stylist: Cole Croghan

Creative Director: Kim Phillips
Graphic Design: Carlisle Publishing Services
Director of Photography: Catrice Tkadlec
Food Photography: Guy Rogers

First Printing

Manufactured in the United States of America

CONTENTS

the Five Commandments of GRILLING

1 *Thou Shalt Be Prepared*

Review the menu, and prepare the ingredients prior to grilling. When prepping your ingredients, keep in mind that cooking times vary according to type of food, size, cooking method, coal temperature and weather conditions.

2 *Thou Shalt Gather Supplies Prior to Grilling*

Assemble what you need on a tray. Such items include: seasonings, sauces, a water-mist bottle, long-handled tongs, basting brush, mitts and a timer. For quick cleanup, line the bottom of the grill with heavy-duty aluminum foil. Make sure that the foil does not cover the holes in the bottom of the grill.

3 *Thou Shalt Examine the Grill*

Before you start the grill, check for adequate fuel (charcoal, wood or propane). For the average fire, expect to use three to four pounds of charcoal. Always store charcoal in a dry location.

4 *Thou Shalt Protect Thy Food*

Prior to lighting the grill, brush or spray the grid (or wire grilling basket) with a light coat of vegetable oil. If you prepare your ingredients in small pieces, they may slip through the basket or grid. An alternative is to place the pieces on skewers.

5 *Thou Shalt Be Aware of Weather Conditions*

If it is cold or windy, increase cooking time, and plan on using additional fuel. Attempt to locate the grill downwind from your gathering. Your guests will appreciate not being smothered in smoke.

GRILLING *guide*

The following guidelines are based on information provided by the Meat Board Test Kitchens and Beef Industry Council.

- *Bell Peppers: Cut peppers into quarters or halves. Remove seeds. Grill 12 to 15 minutes.*
- *Eggplant: Cut small eggplants in half, or cut larger ones in half lengthwise and then into chunks. Grill 10 to 12 minutes, or until tender.*
- *Mushrooms: Grill whole mushrooms (at least 1 1/2 inches in diameter) 10 to 12 minutes.*
- *Onions: Halve or quarter, and grill 12 to 15 minutes.*
- *Potatoes: Parboil small new potatoes 6 to 8 minutes, or until almost tender when tested with a fork. Rinse in cold water; drain well. Grill 10 to 15 minutes on skewers.*
- *Sweet Potatoes: Cut potatoes into 1/2-inch-thick slices. Grill approximately 12 to 14 minutes.*
- *Squash: Cut medium squash in half and then into quarters, or cook small whole ones intact for 10 to 12 minutes.*
- *Cherry Tomatoes, Whole Green Onions: Need to cook only 3 to 5 minutes to be done.*
- *Corn: To grill whole ears, pull husks back, and remove corn silk. Do not pull husks off the cob. Do not brush with oil. Arrange husks back the way they were. Soak in cold water 1 to 2 hours. Wrap in foil, if desired, or grill in husks only 20 to 30 minutes, turning frequently. Fold husks back to end of cob, and use them as handles.*

Guide to Grilling Seafood

- *For grilling whole fish – such as snapper, trout or salmon – use a hinged wire grill basket. The basket also works perfectly for grilling fillets of tender fish, such as perch, snapper, catfish or flounder.*
- *Tuna, salmon or shark can be cooked directly on the grill if handled carefully. Be sure to place small shellfish like shrimp or scallops on metal or water-soaked wooden skewers.*
- *When grilling shellfish in the shell – such as oysters, mussels and clams - place them directly on the hottest part of the grill. They're done when the shell opens. If the shell doesn't open in 5 minutes, throw them away.*
- *There is always the danger of cooking fish too quickly, and you will find it much easier to slow down the cooking time and not overcook the fish if you grill the fillets over medium to medium-low heat.*
- *Turn fish only once since flipping them back and forth tends to break the fish apart.*
- *Allow fish to soak up the flavor of a marinade for at least 30 minutes. Refrigerate while soaking in marinade.*

Tips for Grilling Steaks

- *Tender cuts of beef – such as sirloin, flank steak, top round, tenderloins or steaks – are the prime choices for grilling.*
- *Never add salt to the meat until after it is grilled. Salt tends to dry out the meat and can toughen it.*
- *Use rubs, marinades, sauces and butters to add an extra dimension of flavor. Even basic sea salt or cracked black pepper adds a great taste to beef.*
- *Tongs are the most important tool in the griller's workshop. They allow you to turn the steaks without stabbing them.*
- *Let the steak rest for a couple of minutes after removing it from the grill. This lets the juices redistribute themselves before you cut into the meat.*
- *Rare and medium-rare steaks must cook fast over high heat to sear the outside and, at the same time, keep the inside on the rare side.*
- *Medium to medium-well steaks need to cook slower and on lower heat to allow the outside to brown and thus cook the inside to medium without burning the steaks.*

Vegetable Bruschetta

1 sourdough bread baguette cut diagonally into 20 slices

1/2 cup balsamic vinaigrette dressing

1 small yellow squash or zucchini, cut lengthwise into 1/4-inch-thick slices

25 fresh basil leaves

8 large plum tomatoes, each cut lengthwise into 3 slices

1 1/3 cups shredded cheese

1. *Preheat grill to medium-heat.*
2. *Brush both sides of bread slices with dressing.*
3. *Cut squash slices crosswise in half; place evenly on bread slices. Top with basil and tomatoes. Sprinkle evenly with cheese. Place on grate of the grill.*
4. *Cook 6-8 minutes, or until cheese is melted.*
5. *Serve immediately.*

Serves: 10. Per serving: Calories 170, Fat 8g, Saturated Fat 3 g, Cholesterol 10 mg, Carbohydrate 19 g, Fiber 2 g, Protein 6 g, Sodium 410 mg.

Confetti Vegetables

8 to 10 cherry tomatoes, halved
1 1/2 cups corn, cut from the cob
1 sweet red pepper, julienned
1/2 medium green pepper, julienned
1 small onion, sliced
1 tablespoon fresh basil leaves, chopped
1/4 teaspoon grated lemon rind
Salt, to taste
Pepper, to taste
1 tablespoon unsalted butter

1 *Combine all ingredients, except butter, in a large bowl; toss gently to mix well.*

2 *Divide vegetable mixture in half.*

3 *Place each half in center of a 12-inch × 12-inch piece of heavy-duty aluminum foil.*

4 *Dot vegetables with butter.*

5 *Bring corners of foil together to form a pyramid; twist to seal.*

6 *Grill packets over medium hot coals for 15-20 minutes, or until vegetables are tender.*

7 *Serve immediately.*

Serves: 4. Per serving: Calories 132, Fat 4.1 g, Saturated Fat 2 g, Cholesterol 8 mg, Sodium 94 mg, Carbohydrate 20.7 g, Fiber 4 g, Protein 3.4 g.

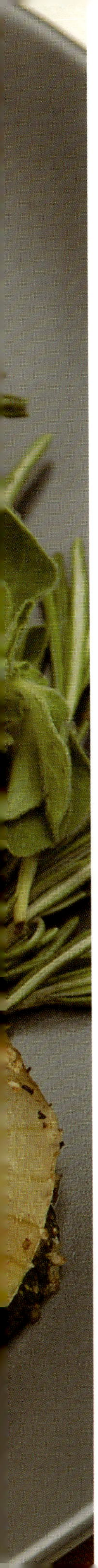

Grilled Mixed Vegetables

2 medium zucchini, sliced into 1/4-inch slices
2 tomatoes, sliced
1 medium onion, thinly sliced
4 teaspoons butter, melted
4 teaspoons Parmesan cheese
1/2 teaspoon rosemary, fresh
1/2 teaspoon thyme
1/2 teaspoon black pepper
1/8 teaspoon oregano
Bread crumbs

1. *Tear off four large squares of double thick foil, and place 1/4 of vegetables in middle of each.*
2. *Melt butter; add cheese and seasonings. Pour over vegetables.*
3. *Sprinkle each individual package with bread crumbs, and seal foil edges tightly.*
4. *Grill over medium hot coals about 15 minutes.*
5. *Turn over and cook 20 minutes more, or until soft.*

Serves: 4. Per serving; Calories 320, Fat 6.5 g, Saturated Fat 3.2 g, Cholesterol 11 mg, Sodium 1633 mg, Carbohydrate 53.9 g, Fiber 5.6 g, Protein 11.6 g.

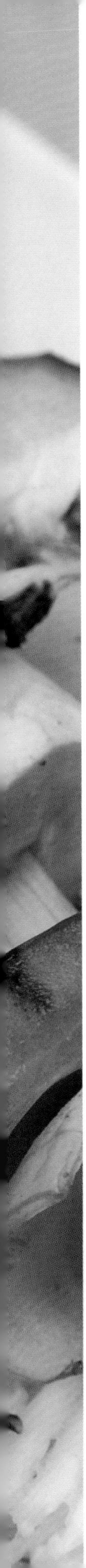

Oriental Grilled Vegetables

1 tablespoon coriander seeds
2 tablespoons soy sauce
1 tablespoon dry sherry
1 tablespoon honey
2 teaspoons ginger, fresh, minced
1 teaspoon chili powder
1 1/2 tablespoon garlic
1 yellow squash, cut into 1-inch slices
1 large onion, cut into 8 wedges
1 red bell pepper, cut into 8 wedges
1 green bell pepper, cut into 8 wedges

1. *Pre-heat the grill.*
2. *Put coriander seeds into a medium bowl, and crush, using the back of a spoon.*
3. *Add the soy sauce, sherry, honey, ginger, oil and garlic.*
4. *Add the vegetables and toss. Let stand for five minutes.*
5. *String the vegetables onto four six-inch skewers.*
6. *Cook 4 inches from the heat source, 3 minutes per side, brushing once with marinade.*

Serves: 4. Per serving: Calories 87, Fat 0.8 g, Saturated fat, 0.1 g, Cholesterol, 0 mg, Sodium, 514 mg, Carbohydrate 17 g, Fiber 3.6 g, Protein 2.8 g.

Barbecued Vegetable Skewers With Garlic-Basil Vinaigrette

For Vinaigrette

3 tablespoons olive oil
3 tablespoons red wine vinegar
3 cloves garlic, minced
1 tablespoon finely chopped fresh basil
1 tablespoon finely chopped fresh rosemary, oregano, sage, marjoram or thyme
1/2 teaspoon salt
1/2 teaspoon pepper

Vegetables

2 pounds of mixed vegetables, such as mushrooms; green, yellow and red pepper strips; slender eggplant, zucchini or yellow squash slices; asparagus spears; baby carrots; halved new potatoes; quartered ears of corn or onion wedges

1 *In a medium bowl, stir all ingredients for vinaigrette (except olive oil) until well mixed. Slowly whisk in olive oil. Cover and refrigerate one hour.*

2 *On wooden skewers, alternate the different vegetables. If using small skewers, place 3 to 4 items; on larger skewers, place 6 items.*

3 *Arrange vegetables on skewers directly over medium-hot coals; cook uncovered for 10 minutes, brushing frequently with vinaigrette.*

Serves: 8. Per serving: Calories 140, Fat 11 gm, Saturated Fat 2 gm, Protein 2 gm, Carbohydrate 9 gm, Fiber 4 gm, Cholesterol 0 mg, Sodium 390 mg.

Grilled Banana Delight

4 bananas
1/2 cup miniature marshmallows
1/2 cup salted peanuts
1/4 cup coconut flakes
1 square semi-sweet baking chocolate, chopped
1/2 cup thawed whipped topping

1. *Preheat grill to medium-high heat.*
2. *Peel bananas. Cut lengthwise to within 1/2 inch of each end.*
3. *Place on large sheet of heavy-duty foil.*
4. *Top evenly with marshmallows, peanuts, coconut and chocolate. Roll up foil loosely.*
5. *Grill 5-7 minutes, or until bananas are softened.*
6. *Place 1 banana on each dessert plate. Top evenly with whipped topping.*

Serves: 4. Per serving: Calories 33, Fat 16 g, Saturated Fat, 7 g, Cholesterol 0 mg, Fiber 5 g, Carbohydrate 46 g, Sodium 105 mg.

Apple-Glazed Pork Kabobs

- 2 tablespoons lemon juice
- Salt, to taste
- 1 pound boneless pork loin, cut into 1-inch cubes
- 1 cup apple jelly
- 1 teaspoon cinnamon
- 2 tablespoons unsalted butter

1. *Sprinkle lemon juice and salt evenly over pork cubes.*
2. *In small saucepan, make glaze by mixing together the jelly, lemon juice, cinnamon and butter.*
3. *Simmer until well blended.*
4. *Thread pork onto skewers, and spoon glaze over all.*
5. *Grill over hot coals 10-12 minutes, turning and basting frequently.*

Serves: 4. Per serving: Calories 274, Fat 12.7 g, Saturated Fat 5.9 g, Cholesterol, 78 mg, Sodium, 128 mg, Carbohydrate 14.6 g, Fiber 1.1 g, Protein 25.3 g.

Chicken Little Kabobs

1/4 cup brown sugar
1/2 cup dry sherry
1/4 cup soy sauce
4 chicken breasts
3 cups zucchini
1/2 cup pineapple chunks
2 onions, quartered
Salt, to taste
Pepper, to taste

1. *Mix sugar, sherry and soy sauce in 1 quart saucepan.*
2. *Cook over medium heat, stirring until sugar dissolves; cool.*
3. *Cut chicken breasts into chunks.*
4. *Place chicken chunks in glass dish; pour mixture over chicken.*
5. *Cover; refrigerate at least 3 hours, turning occasionally. Drain chicken; save marinade.*
6. *Place chicken, vegetables and pineapple on skewers.*
7. *Grill until done.*
8. *Sprinkle with salt and pepper.*

Serves: 4. Per serving: Calories 359, Fat 3 g, Saturated Fat, 0.7 g, Cholesterol 131 mg, Sodium 904 mg, Carbohydrate 27.8 g, Fiber 3 g, Protein 55.3 g.

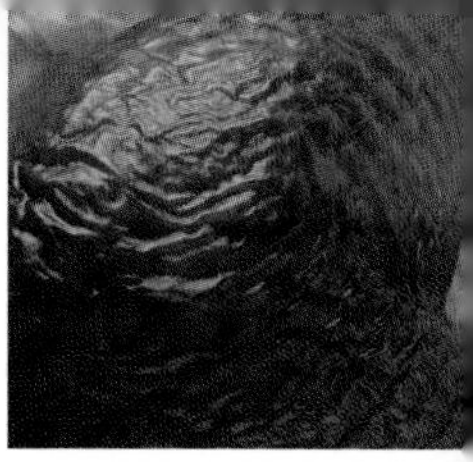

Hickory Smoked Turkey

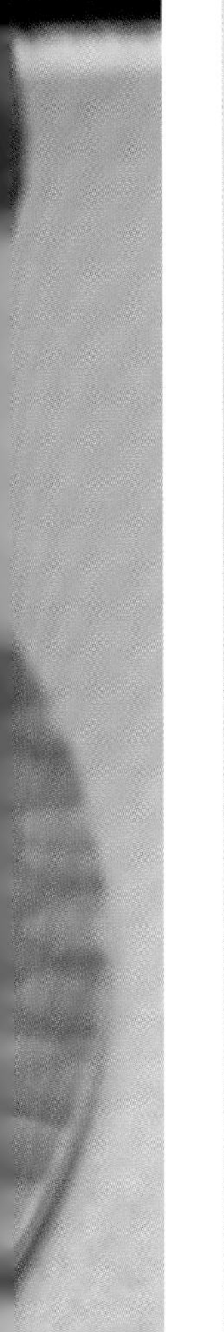

2 quarts apple juice
3 quarts water
1 pound brown sugar
1 cup salt
3 oranges, quartered
4 ounces fresh ginger, thinly sliced
15 whole cloves
6 bay leaves
6 large cloves garlic, crushed
1 (12- to 14-pound) turkey
3 tablespoons olive oil

1. *In a large saucepan over high heat, bring the apple juice, brown sugar and salt to a boil, stirring to dissolve the sugar and salt.*
2. *Cook for 1 minute; remove from heat and skim off the foam. Allow the mixture to cool to room temperature.*
3. *In a container large enough to hold the turkey, combine 3 quarts of water, oranges, ginger, cloves, bay leaves and garlic. Add the juice mixture, and stir.*
4. *Remove and discard giblets from the turkey cavity. Rinse the turkey inside and out; drain and submerge it in brine. (If necessary, top turkey with a heavy weight to make sure it is completely immersed.) Refrigerate for 24 hours.*
5. *Soak the hickory-wood chips in water for at least 30 minutes, and let dry prior to placing in the grill. Follow the grill's instructions for using wood chips. Set up the grill for indirect cooking over medium heat.*
6. *Remove the turkey from brine, and pat dry with paper towels. Tie the legs together with cotton string. Lightly brush turkey with olive oil, and place on a roasting rack set inside a heavy-gauge foil pan. Cook indirectly over medium heat.*
7. *When the wings are golden brown (about 40 minutes), wrap them with aluminum foil to prevent burning. Brush the rest of the turkey with more olive oil.*
8. *When the turkey breasts are golden brown (about 1 hour), cover the remainder of the turkey with aluminum foil to prevent the skin from becoming too dark. The turkey is done when its juices run clear, when the internal temperature of the thickest part of the thigh is approximately 180 degrees and when the internal temperature of the breast reaches 170 degrees on a food thermometer.*

Serves: 8. Per serving: Calories, 1,382, Fat 56 g, Saturated Fat 14 g, Protein 112 g, Carbohydrate 108 g, Fiber 8 g, Cholesterol 420 mg, Sodium 1, 215 mg.

Pork in the Garden Salad

2/3 pound red potatoes, cut into 1/8-inch-thick slices
1/2 tablespoon extra virgin olive oil, divided
Cooking spray
1 small zucchini, cut lengthwise into 1/4-inch-thick slices
1 medium yellow squash, cut lengthwise into 1/4-inch-thick slices
1 large red bell pepper, quartered
1 large orange bell pepper, quartered
1 medium red onion, cut into 1/4-inch-thick slices
4 (1-ounce) slices sourdough bread
1 garlic clove, peeled and halved
8 ounces roast pork, thinly sliced
1 1/2 tablespoons white wine vinegar
1 tablespoon honey
1 teaspoon chopped fresh oregano
1 teaspoon Dijon mustard
3/4 teaspoon salt
1/2 teaspoon chopped fresh thyme
1/4 teaspoon black pepper

1. *Prepare grill.*
2. *Toss potatoes with 1 teaspoon oil. Place potatoes on grill rack coated with cooking spray. Grill 4 minutes on each side, or until tender.*
3. *Place zucchini, squash, bell peppers and onion on grill rack. Cook 3 minutes on each side.*
4. *Place bread slices on grill rack. Grill 1 minute on each side, or until well marked. Rub both sides of each bread slice with cut sides of garlic.*
5. *Coarsely chop zucchini, squash and bell peppers.*
6. *Combine vegetables and roasted pork in a large bowl, tossing gently.*
7. *Combine vinegar and remaining ingredients, stirring with a whisk.*
8. *Gradually add remaining 3 1/2 teaspoons oil, stirring with a whisk. Drizzle vinegar mixture over vegetable mixture, tossing to coat.*
9. *Serve bread with salad.*

Serves: 4. Per serving: Calories 310, Fat 8.5 g, Saturated Fat 1.7 g, Protein 15 g, Cholesterol 26 mg, Fiber 5.6 g, Carbohydrate 45.1 g, Sodium 755 mg.

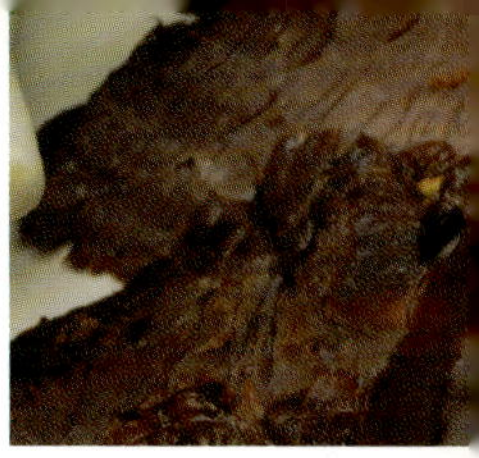

Arizona London Broil

1 bottle low sodium soy sauce
1 tablespoon diced fresh ginger
1 jalapeno, diced
1 (4-6 pound) London broil
4 cups barbecue sauce

1. *Mix soy sauce, ginger and jalapeno together.*
2. *Marinate meat overnight in mixture.*
3. *Brush on barbecue sauce.*
4. *Cook over mesquite coals for 2 1/2 to 3 hours, or until desired doneness.*

Serves: 8. Per serving: Calories 541, Fat 29.5 g, Saturated Fat 10.9 g, Cholesterol, 144 mg, Sodium 2091 mg, Carbohydrate 19 g, Fiber 1.8 g, Protein, 50 g.

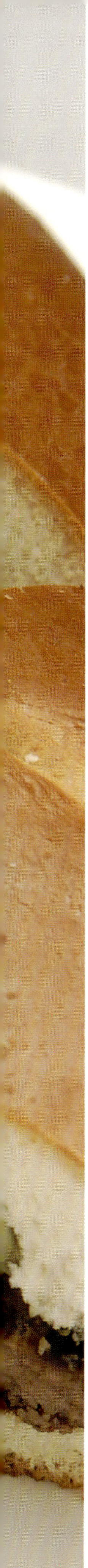

Grande Beef Burger

1 pound ground beef
1 teaspoon ground cumin
1 teaspoon salt
1 (4-ounce) can chopped green chilies, drained
3 ounces Monterey Jack cheese, cut into 6 slices
1 (1.5-pound) round loaf sourdough bread
2 tablespoons unsalted butter
1 cup shredded lettuce
1 small tomato, chopped
2 green onions with tops, thinly sliced
2 tablespoons sliced pitted ripe olives
1/2 cup sour cream
Guacamole (optional)

1. *Combine ground beef, cumin and salt, mixing lightly but thoroughly.*
2. *Line 9-inch round pan with plastic wrap or aluminum foil.*
3. *Divide beef mixture into 2 equal portions; shape 1 portion into large patty by pressing meat lightly but firmly into pan.*
4. *Remove patty; place on lightly greased flat baking sheet.*
5. *Sprinkle chilies evenly over patty; arrange cheese over chilies.*
6. *Shape remaining beef mixture into large patty; place over first patty.*
7. *Press edges together securely to seal.*
8. *Place burger on grill over medium hot coals.*
9. *Cover cooker; grill 7 minutes.*
10. *To turn, slide lightly greased flat baking sheet under burger.*
11. *Hold another flat baking sheet over burger; flip over and carefully slide uncooked side back onto grill.*
12. *Continue grilling, covered, 7 minutes, or to desired doneness. Remove burger from grill with flat baking sheet.*
13. *Meanwhile, slice bread loaf horizontally in half to form a bun.*
14. *Remove soft bread from inside top half of bun, leaving 1/2-inch to 1-inch thick shell.*
15. *Spread cut sides of bun with butter; toast cut sides on grill 1 minute.*
16. *Place burger on bottom half of bun.*
17. *Arrange lettuce, tomato, green onions and olives on top of burger; cover with top of bun; cut into wedges.*
18. *Serve sour cream and guacamole, if desired, with burger.*
19. *If using an open grill, increase cooking time 3 minutes.*

Serves: 4. Per serving: Calories 953, Fat 43 g, Saturated Fat 21.7 g, Cholesterol 115 mg, Sodium 2000 mg, Carbohydrate 97.6 g, Fiber 7.1 g, Protein 43.4 g.

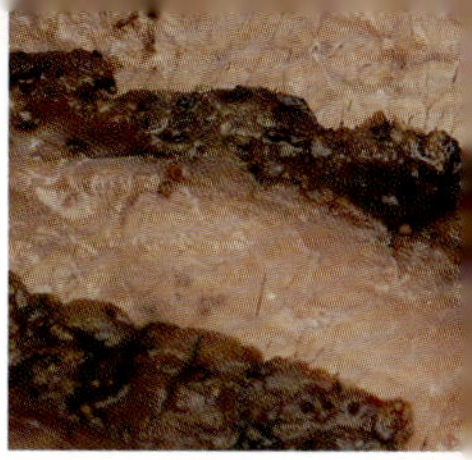

Heat 'N' Sweet Brisket

1 large beef brisket, boneless chuck
1 cup salad oil
4 tablespoons black pepper
2 ounces fresh garlic
6 bay leaves
1 teaspoon salt
1 cup honey

1. *Trim the fat off the meat.*
2. *Mix all ingredients together, and pour over the meat.*
3. *Refrigerate 24-28 hours, turning morning and night.*
4. *Grill meat 6-10 hours to the side of a moderate wood fire.*
5. *Turn meat occasionally, basting with the reserved marinade.*
6. *This can be baked in the oven, covered, at 250 degrees for 6-10 hours, or until tender.*

Serves: 8. Per serving: Calories 744, Fat 43.8 g, Saturated Fat 9.5 g, Cholesterol 144 mg, Sodium 479 mg, Carbohydrate 39.6 g, Fiber 1.1 g, Protein 48 g.

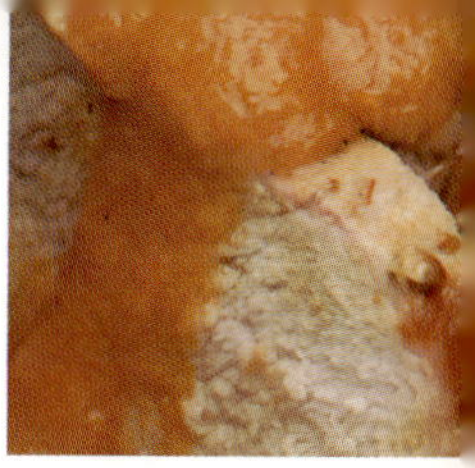

Peachy Smoked Pork Roast

1/2 teaspoon salt
1/2 teaspoon black pepper
1 teaspoon ginger
2 tablespoons vegetable oil
1/2 cup brown sugar
3 tablespoons chili sauce
1 (29-ounce) can peach slices in heavy syrup, undrained
2 pound pork loin roast

1. *In blender, combine salt, pepper, ginger, oil, vinegar, brown sugar, chili sauce and undrained peaches. Blend until smooth.*

2. *Place pork loin in a heavy plastic bag; pour on half of peach sauce. Refrigerate, covered, overnight. Refrigerate remaining peach sauce.*

3. *Prepare grill by arranging a drip pan surrounded by medium hot coals. If using gas grill, heat to medium temperature.*

4. *Add hickory chips, dampened with water, to heat source.*

5. *Place pork, meat thermometer inserted, on grill over drip pan. Baste often with marinade until internal temperature reaches 155 degrees, about 45-60 minutes.*

6. *Let stand 10 minutes, allowing internal temperature to rise to 160 degrees.*

7. *Slice thinly and serve with reserved peach sauce, heated.*

Serves: 6. Per serving: Calories 489, Fat 24.1 g, Saturated Fat 7 g, Cholesterol 101 mg, Sodium 338 mg, Carbohydrate 36.8 g, Fiber 1.6 g, Protein 31.2 g.

Rack of Lamb with Raspberry Mint Sauce

2 pounds rack of lamb (rib roast)
1/4 teaspoon oregano
2 tablespoons chopped fresh rosemary
2 teaspoons salt
1/4 teaspoon allspice
3 large cloves garlic, finely chopped
1 teaspoon black pepper
1/2 teaspoon dried leaf thyme
2 lemon peels, finely grated
1 (12-ounce) bottle barbecue sauce
3 tablespoons mint sauce

1. *Have butcher trim rack of lamb, removing all visible fat and thin flap of meat on the end of the rib.*
2. *Also, have the butcher cut through the chime bone.*
3. *Cut and scrape meat from between long rib bones, leaving 2 inches to 3 inches of clean bone protruding.*
4. *Cover exposed bone with a double layer of foil to keep from burning.*
5. *In a small bowl, combine oregano, rosemary, salt, allspice, garlic, pepper, thyme and lemon peel.*
6. *Rub mixture over surface of lamb; cover and refrigerate at least 2 hours.*
7. *Place lamb on grill at opposite end from coals; smoke for about 1 1/2 to 2 hours. Fire should be medium.*
8. *Mix barbecue and mint sauce in a pan, and simmer for 10 minutes.*
9. *Serve warm with lamb.*

Serves: 4. Per serving: Calories 471, Fat 22.5 g, Saturated Fat 7.7 g, Cholesterol 152 mg, Sodium 2113 mg, Carbohydrate 19.6 g, Fiber 1.7 g, Protein 47.3 g.

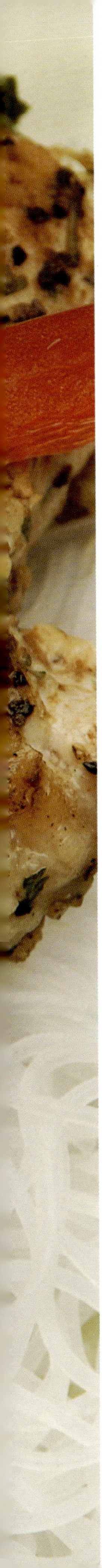

Asian Peppered Chicken

4 chicken breasts
2 tablespoons minced garlic
2 tablespoons fresh grated ginger
1 bunch cilantro, with roots
1 1/2 teaspoons black pepper
6 tablespoons Asian tamarind sauce

1. *Wash skin and prick chicken breasts with a knife tip or skewer.*
2. *Chop garlic, ginger and cilantro; combine.*
3. *Add pepper to dry marinade.*
4. *Toss with chicken in a bowl to coat; refrigerate 2-4 hours.*
5. *Grill over charcoal 5 minutes. Start basting with tamarind sauce. The chicken will take on a mahogany brown color. Turn and baste frequently.*
6. *Grill 15 minutes.*

Serves: 4. Per serving: Calories 282, Fat 3 g, Saturated Fat 0.8 g, Cholesterol 131 mg, Sodium 223 mg, Carbohydrate 10.7 g, Fiber 0.7 g, Protein 53.1 g.

Chicken Monterey

2 tablespoons canola oil
6 boneless chicken breasts
2 tablespoons teriyaki sauce
12 ounces barbecue sauce
6 slices Monterey Jack cheese
6 slices hickory smoked bacon, cooked

1. *Brush chicken liberally with oil, and sprinkle with seasoning.*
2. *Grill chicken over medium coals 10 minutes each side, or until done.*
3. *Mix teriyaki and barbecue sauce to form glaze.*
4. *Cover chicken with glaze, top with cheese and slice of bacon, and cook until cheese begins to melt.*
5. *Pour remaining glaze in serving dish, and place chicken on top.*

Serves: 6. Per serving: Calories 731, Fat 41.4 g, Saturated Fat 16.8 g, Cholesterol 205 mg, Sodium 2,226 mg, Carbohydrate 12.4 g, Fiber 0.8 g, Protein 77.2 g.

Lime Chicken Breasts

4 chicken breast halves, deboned and skinned
2 tablespoons butter

Marinade

1/4 cup lime juice
1/4 teaspoon salt
1/8 teaspoon black pepper
1/2 teaspoon dried dillweed
1/2 teaspoon dried minced onion

1 *Combine all marinade ingredients in heavy zip-lock plastic bag; mix.*

2 *Add chicken breasts; seal bag. Turn to coat chicken with marinade; let stand at room temperature 10-15 minutes.*

3 *Meanwhile, preheat charcoal grill.*

4 *Place chicken breasts over medium coals or low-setting on gas grill. Cover; grill 5 minutes on each side.*

5 *Baste with butter after turning.*

Cook's Suggestion: Serve hot with buttered noodles.

Serves: 4. Per serving: Calories 407, Fat 13.9 g, Saturated Fat 5.9 g, Cholesterol 209 mg, Sodium 316 mg, Carbohydrate 0.1 g, Fiber 0 g, Protein 70.5 g.

Smoked Chicken Quarters

1/8 teaspoon salt
4 chicken breasts
basil leaves and capers to garnish

Sauce

2 cups fresh basil leaves
5 tablespoons red wine vinegar
5 anchovy fillets, chopped
2 tablespoons Dijon mustard
3/4 teaspoon salt
3/4 cup olive oil
1/4 cup corn oil
1/2 teaspoon freshly ground pepper

1. *Lightly salt each chicken quarter.*
2. *Smoke over hickory wood for 2 1/2 hours at 225 degrees.*
3. *Place first 5 sauce ingredients in food processor for 30 seconds.*
4. *With machine running, gradually add oils through feed tube, and blend until sauce is thick.*
5. *Mix in pepper.*
6. *Transfer to small serving bowl; let stand at room temperature.*
7. *Serve sauce on the side of chicken, and garnish with basil leaves and capers.*

Serves: 4. Per serving: Calories 746, Fat 57.3 g, Saturated Fat 8 g, Cholesterol 131 mg, Sodium 1684 mg, Carbohydrate 3.9 g, Fiber 2 g, Protein 53.7 g.

South of the Border Grilled Chicken Salad

1/4 cup soy sauce
1 cup water
1 lime, juiced
1/8 teaspoon garlic powder
1 teaspoon freshly ground pepper, divided
4 chicken breasts
8 cups torn lettuce
1/2 cup grated cucumber
3/4 cup hot or mild salsa
1/4 cup cucumber salad dressing
1 green pepper, sliced into thin rings
2 green onions, thinly sliced
2 tomatoes, cut into wedges
Fresh parsley sprigs
3 green onions, chopped

Glazed Pecans
1 cup pecans, halved
1/4 cup brown sugar
1/4 teaspoon salt

1 *Mix soy sauce, water, lime juice, garlic powder and 1/2 teaspoon pepper.*

2 *Add chicken and marinate in refrigerator 6-24 hours.*

3 *Grill chicken over charcoal just until done, but not dry.*

4 *Slice diagonally into 2-inch strips, and season with remaining pepper.*

5 *Chill until serving time.*

6 *For glazed pecans, combine pecans, sugar, water and salt in small saucepan.*

7 *Cook over medium high heat, 5-10 minutes, stirring constantly until syrup has changed to crystals and pecans are evenly coated.*

8 *Spread on cookie sheet, and bake in 225-degree oven for 45 minutes to 1 hour.*

9 *To assemble salad on large platter, layer in this order: lettuce, grated cucumber, salsa, salad dressing, chicken, green pepper rings, green onion slices and glazed pecans.*

10 *Garnish with tomato wedges, fresh parsley sprigs and green onion tops.*

Serves: 4. Per serving: Calories 611, Fat 39 g, Saturated Fat 5.7 g, Cholesterol 76 mg, Sodium 1143 mg, Carbohydrate 35.1 g, Fiber 6.5 g, Protein 29.8 g.

Rio Grande Chicken

1/4 cup milk
1 cup yellow cornmeal
4 tablespoons mild or hot salsa
6 chicken breasts
1/4 cup melted butter

1. *Prepare grill.*
2. *Pour milk into pie plate.*
3. *On waxed paper, combine corn meal and salsa; mix well.*
4. *Dip chicken pieces into milk, then into corn meal mixture, coating all sides.*
5. *Cover the grill with foil first, then place the chicken breasts on the foil.*
6. *Grill 30-45 minutes, turning twice.*

Serves: 6. Per serving: Calories 538, Fat 29.3 g, Saturated Fat 11 g, Cholesterol 168 mg, Sodium 209 mg, Carbohydrate 18.9 g, Fiber 1.7 g, Protein 49.9 g.

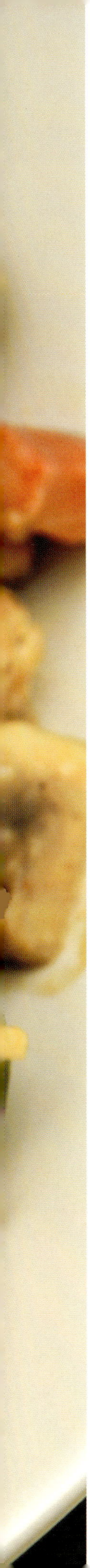

Shrimp Monica with Grilled Vegetables

3 tablespoons extra virgin olive oil
1 teaspoon dried basil
1 teaspoon dried thyme
2 small, firm zucchini, cut into 3/8-inch slices
1 red bell pepper, cored and halved
1 green bell pepper, cored and halved
1/2 pound mushrooms
2 bunches green onions
1 1/2 pounds medium shrimp
1/2 pound butter
1 tablespoon flour
1 1/2 tablespoons Creole seasoning
1 cup half and half
8 ounces tomato sauce
1 cup grated Romano cheese
1 cup grated Parmigiano-Reggiano cheese
1 pound angel hair pasta

1. *Combine olive oil, basil and thyme in a large baking dish or mixing bowl.*
2. *Using your hands or a brush, gently dip or coat vegetables with olive oil mixture; set aside.*
3. *Shell and devein shrimp. Set aside while preparing grill.*
4. *For best flavor, grill vegetables and shrimp over mesquite wood chips. Wood chips may be mixed with traditional charcoal briquettes.*
5. *Make a roux by melting butter and flour in a large skillet or saucepan over medium heat, stirring constantly.*
6. *Add Creole seasoning, half and half and tomato sauce. Continue stirring, reduce heat and simmer gently until sauce thickens, 4-6 minutes. When you are ready to serve, gently re-warm sauce, add cheeses and mix thoroughly.*
7. *Meanwhile, boil water for pasta, and cook according to package directions.*
8. *Grill vegetables and shrimp over medium-hot coals, 3-5 minutes on each side.*
9. *When vegetables are cooked, carefully chop them into bite-size pieces. Toss vegetables, shrimp, cooked pasta and sauce together in a large mixing bowl.*
10. *Serve immediately.*

Serves: 8. Per serving: Calories 730, Fat 41 g, Saturated Fat 22 g, Protein 37 g, Carbohydrate 56 g, Fiber 4 g, Cholesterol 230 mg, Sodium 1,030 mg.

Cedar-Planked Salmon

1 untreated cedar plank (14 × 7 × 1 inch)
1/2 cup sun-dried tomato vinaigrette dressing
1/4 cup finely chopped fresh parsley
1/4 cup finely chopped sun-dried tomatoes
1 tablespoon vegetable oil
2 pounds salmon fillet, cut 1-inch thick with skin removed

1. *Immerse the plank in water, placing a weight on top of the plank to keep it submerged. Soak at least 4 hours, or overnight.*
2. *Preheat the grill to medium heat. Mix dressing, parsley and tomatoes. Set aside.*
3. *Brush top of cedar plank with oil. Top with salmon.*
4. *Place plank with salmon on grill. Cover with lid.*
5. *Grill for 10 minutes.*
6. *Brush with dressing mixture; continue grilling 10 minutes, or until salmon flakes easily with fork.*

Serves: 8. Per serving: Calories 170, Fat 6 g, Saturated Fat 1 g, Cholesterol 60 mg, Carbohydrate 3 g, Fiber 0 g, Protein 23 g, Sodium 280 mg.

Barbecued Red Snapper

4 fillets red snapper
1 small onion, chopped
1/4 teaspoon ground cloves
1 tablespoon brown sugar
1 teaspoon chili powder
1/4 cup cider vinegar
1/4 teaspoon cayenne pepper
2 tablespoons catsup
2 tablespoons dry mustard
1 teaspoon Worcestershire sauce

1. *Combine all ingredients, except snapper, in a pot, place over medium heat and boil until reduced to a thin syrup.*
2. *Pour syrup through a strainer, discard the cooked ingredients in the strainer and chill the marinade.*
3. *Place snapper fillets in a baking dish, and spoon some marinade over them, coating all sides.*
4. *Marinate in the refrigerator for 1 hour. Pour off marinade into a small pan, and heat to boiling.*
5. *Grill the snapper over hot coals, basting with a teaspoon of the marinade on each side.*
6. *Remove snapper when internal temperature reaches 155 degrees, or the fish is just flaky, and the translucent color is gone.*

Serves: 4. Per serving: Calories 266, Fat 4.6 g, Saturated Fat 0.7 g, Cholesterol 81 mg, Sodium 243 mg, Carbohydrate 9.6 g, Fiber 1.3 g, Protein 46.4 g.

Thai Styled Salmon

4 fillets salmon, boneless and skinless
1 teaspoon salt
1 teaspoon black pepper

Thai-Style Vegetables

Vegetable oil
1 red bell pepper, julienned
1 summer squash, small and tender, chopped
2 green onions, coarsely chopped
2 celery stalks, julienned
1/2 cup finely chopped shallots
1/2 teaspoon salt
1 teaspoon chili powder
1/2 cup fresh copped coriander
1/2 cup fresh chopped mint
1/8 teaspoon sugar
1/2 cup fresh lime juice

1. *To smoke salmon fillets, set smoker at 250 degrees for 20 minutes, using apple wood.*
2. *Place salmon on smoker grills, and liberally sprinkle salt and pepper.*
3. *Place salmon on grills, and prepare vegetables.*
4. *In a medium sauté pan, heat vegetable oil to smoking point.*
5. *Add cut and prepared vegetables together, and sauté quickly.*
6. *Finish with remaining spices and sugar until the vegetables reach desired tenderness.*
7. *Add lime juice just before serving.*

Serves: 4. Per serving: Calories 755, Fat 43.4 g, Saturated Fat 8.6 g, Cholesterol 234 mg, Sodium 1161 mg, Carbohydrate 10.2 g, Fiber 2.3 g, Protein 80.8 g.

Trout Grilled with Wild Rice

- 1 tablespoon olive oil
- 2 cups thinly sliced leek, divided
- 1 1/2 cups sliced mushrooms
- 1 clove garlic, crushed
- 4 cups water
- 1/4 teaspoon salt, divided
- 1/4 teaspoon black pepper, divided
- 1 cup uncooked wild rice
- 4 thyme sprigs
- 4 cleaned brook trout
- 1 tablespoon unsalted butter
- 1 tablespoon chopped fresh parsley
- Additional thyme sprigs

1. *Heat oil in medium saucepan over medium high heat.*
2. *Add 1/4 cup leek, mushrooms and garlic.*
3. *Sauté 3 minutes.*
4. *Add water, rice, 1/8 teaspoon salt, 1/8 teaspoon pepper; bring to a boil. Cover, reduce heat and simmer 50 minutes, or until rice is tender.*
5. *Drain rice, reserving 1 cup cooking liquid; set rice aside. Return cooking liquid to pan. Bring to a boil, and cook 8 minutes, or until reduced to 1/2 cup. Remove from heat; set broth aside, and keep warm.*
6. *Place 1 thyme sprig in the center of each of four (10-inch) squares of aluminum foil.*
7. *Place 1 trout fillet on top of each thyme sprig. Sprinkle remaining salt and pepper over inside cavities of fish.*
8. *Stuff 1/2 cup rice mixture into the cavity of each fish.*
9. *Wrap fish in foil, twisting the ends to seal.*
10. *Prepare grill, and place the foil-wrapped fish on grill rack; grill 10 minutes on each side, or until fish flakes easily when tested with a fork.*
11. *Unwrap fish; remove and discard skin. Set the fish aside, and keep warm.*
12. *Melt butter in a small saucepan over medium-high heat. Add remaining leek, and sauté 2 minutes, or until tender.*
13. *Divide leek evenly among 4 individual plates, and top with fish.*
14. *Drizzle 2 tablespoons broth over each fish, and sprinkle with parsley.*

Serves: 4. Per serving: Calories 384, Fat 10.6 g, Saturated Fat 2.4 g, Cholesterol 79 mg, Sodium 228 mg, Carbohydrates 13.2 g, Fiber 0.6 g, Protein 52 g.

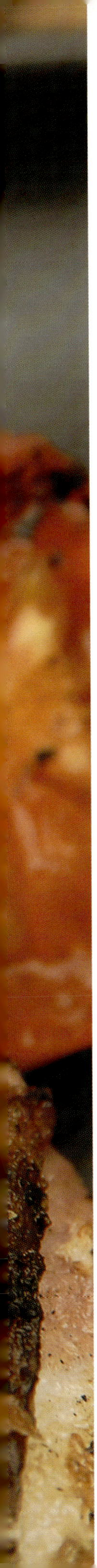

Charcoal Grilled Catfish

6 catfish fillets
1/4 teaspoon salt
1/4 teaspoon black pepper
2 tablespoons vegetable oil
6 slices hickory smoked bacon

1. *Salt and pepper catfish well.*
2. *Brush both sides of fish with vegetable oil.*
3. *Wrap bacon around each piece.*
4. *Place on a wire rack, and grill over charcoal fire until bacon and fish are done.*

Serves: 6. Per serving: Calories 459, Fat 38.5 g, Saturated Fat 11.5 g, cholesterol 100 mg, Sodium 459 mg, Carbohydrate 0.1 g, Fiber 0 g, Protein 28 g.

Citrus Tuna

2 pounds tuna steaks
1 cup orange juice
1 cup grapefruit juice
1/4 cup lime juice
1 teaspoon dried thyme
1/4 teaspoon cayenne pepper
1/4 teaspoon salt
1 tablespoon paprika

1. *Mix juices, sherry, thyme, cayenne pepper and salt in a shallow baking dish.*
2. *Add tuna, and allow to marinate 3-4 hours in refrigerator.*
3. *Preheat and oil grill.*
4. *Remove tuna from marinade.*
5. *Place fish on grill, and sprinkle with paprika. Turn after about 5-7 minutes, and continue cooking for another 5-7 minutes.*

Serves: 4. Per serving: Calories 379, Fat 11.5 g, Saturated Fat 2.9 g, Cholesterol, 85 mg, Sodium 237 mg, Carbohydrate 14.8 g, Fiber 0.8 g, Protein 54 g.

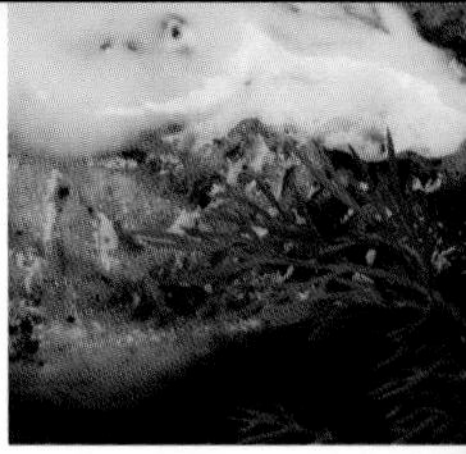

Creamy Dill Salmon

1 cup plain yogurt, divided
3 tablespoons water
1 tablespoon canola oil
1/2 teaspoon dillweed, divided
4 salmon steaks, 1-inch thick
2 tablespoons butter
1 egg, slightly beaten

1 *In a 12-inch × 7-inch baking dish, combine 1/2 cup yogurt, water, oil and 1/4 teaspoon dillweed.*

2 *Add salmon; cover and refrigerate 1 hour.*

3 *Remove salmon from sauce; grill or broil until fish flakes with a fork.*

4 *Meanwhile, in small saucepan, melt butter; stir in remaining yogurt, dillweed and egg. Over low heat, cook and stir until thickened, being careful not to boil.*

5 *Serve creamy dill warm with salmon.*

Serves: 4. Per serving: Calories 804, Fat 47.7 g, Saturated Fat 9.6 g, Cholesterol 239 mg, Sodium 381 mg, Carbohydrate 5 g, Fiber 0 g, Protein 88.4 g.

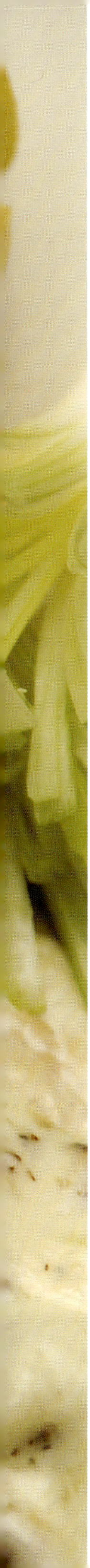

Smoked Trout with Hazelnut Cream Sauce

4 medium trout

Hazelnut Cream Sauce

6 tablespoons unsalted butter

1/2 cup chopped, husked, toasted hazelnuts

3 green onions, sliced

2/3 cup whipping cream, boiled until reduced to 1/3 cup

1 1/2 tablespoons fresh lemon juice

1/4 teaspoon freshly ground pepper

1 *Smoke-cook trout over hickory or apple wood 1 hour at 200 degrees - 1 1/2 hours if frozen.*

2 *About 15 minutes before trout is done, melt butter in large skillet.*

3 *Add hazelnuts and green onions.*

4 *Cook until onions wilt, stirring occasionally, about 3 minutes.*

5 *Add reduced cream, and stir until heated thoroughly.*

6 *Mix in lemon juice, salt and pepper.*

7 *Spoon sauce over smoked trout before serving.*

Serves: 4. Per serving: Calories 574, Fat 50.7 g, Saturated Fat 16.1 g, Cholesterol 108 mg, Sodium 37 mg, Carbohydrate 7.8 g, Fiber 2.7 g, Protein 21.9 g.

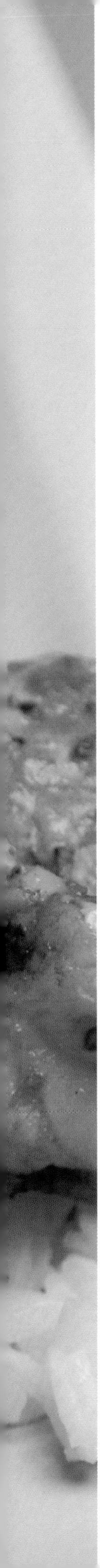

Spicy Shrimp

2 pounds large shrimp, uncooked; remove the skin and tails
1 cup olive oil
1 lemon, juiced
2 tablespoons hot pepper sauce
3 cloves garlic, minced
1 tablespoon tomato paste or catsup
2 teaspoons dried oregano
1 teaspoon salt
1 teaspoon black pepper
1/4 cup fresh cilantro, chopped
1 tablespoon chili powder

1. *In a large bowl, mix together all of the ingredients, except the shrimp.*

2. *Let sit overnight at room temperature in a plastic container, shaking occasionally as the ingredients settle. This will infuse the oil with flavor.*

3. *Dip each shrimp in the marinade to fully coat, and then put all of the shrimp and marinade in a container and place in the refrigerator for several hours, flipping occasionally to properly distribute the marinade.*

4. *While preheating your grill, skewer the shrimp.*

5. *Place on grill for a few minutes, flipping once.*

Serves: 4. Per serving: Calories 736, Fat 58 g, Saturated Fat 8 g, Cholesterol 340 mg, Sodium 980 mg, Carbohydrate 6.7 g, Fiber 0.7 g, Protein 46.8 g.

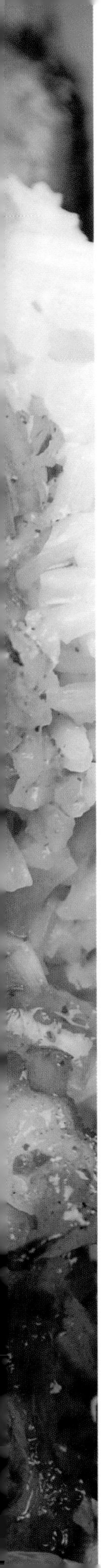

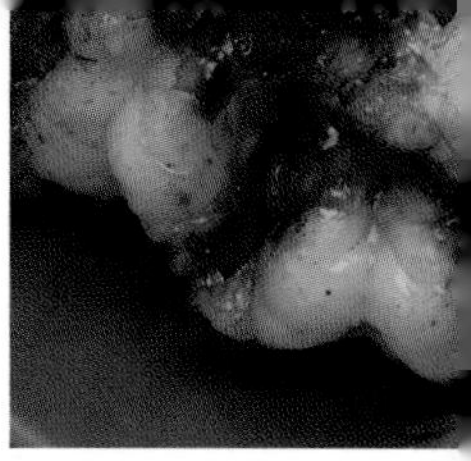

Sweet Maple Shrimp

2 pounds large shrimp, uncooked; remove skin and tails
1 finely chopped onion
1 cup olive oil
1 teaspoon brown sugar
1 teaspoon cayenne papper
1/2 teaspoon salt
1/2 teaspoon oregano
1 teaspoon garlic powder
1/2 cup maple syrup

1. *In a large bowl, mix everything together, and then add shrimp.*
2. *Leave it in the fridge overnight, or at least for several hours.*
3. *Flip occasionally to distribute shrimp marinade. Pull from refrigerator an hour or so before cooking to let things warm and loosen up somewhat.*
4. *On the second day, preheat your grill while skewering the shrimp.*
5. *Place flat on a fine-screen mesh cookware. Be careful because the dripping marinade can cause the flames to blaze up unexpectedly.*
6. *Serve over rice or pasta, or as is.*

Serves: 4. Per serving: Calories 783, Fat 57.9 g, Saturated Fat 8 g, Cholesterol 340 mg, Sodium 634 mg, Carbohydrate 19 g, Fiber 0.7 g, Protein 46.5 g.

Firecracker Grilled Salmon

4 (6-ounce) salmon steak fillets
1/4 cup peanut oil
2 tablespoons soy sauce
2 tablespoons balsamic vinegar
2 tablespoons chopped green onions
1 1/2 teaspoons brown sugar
1 clove garlic, minced
3/4 teaspoon grated ginger
1/2 teaspoon red pepper flakes
1/2 teaspoon sesame oil
1/8 teaspoon salt

1. *Place salmon fillets in a glass dish.*
2. *Whisk together remaining ingredients, and pour over salmon.*
3. *Cover with plastic wrap, and marinate in refrigerator 4-6 hours.*
4. *Remove salmon from marinade, and place on a well-oiled grill 5 inches from coals.*
5. *Grill for 10 minutes per inch of thickness, measured at thickest part, or until salmon just flakes when tested with a fork.*
6. *Turn halfway through cooking.*

Serves: 4. Per serving: Calories 848, Fat 57.1 g, Saturated Fat 11 g, Cholesterol 234 mg, Sodium 575 mg, Carbohydrate 4.1 g, Fiber 0.3 g, Protein 79.4 g.

Honey Fired Bass

4 fillets bass

Marinade

1/2 cup white wine
1 cup soy sauce
4 tablespoons honey
1/2 cup vegetable oil
1 teaspoon grated ginger

1. *Combine all marinade ingredients.*
2. *Pour over bass, and set in refrigerator to marinate 1-2 hours.*
3. *Remove; grill over medium coals 3-5 minutes per side.*
4. *Baste with marinade while grilling.*
5. *Garnish with lemon wedges.*

Serves: 4. Per serving: Calories 427, Fat 30.1 g, Cholesterol 54 mg, Sodium 2,181 mg, Carbohydrate 20.8 g, Fiber 0 g, Protein 18.4 g.

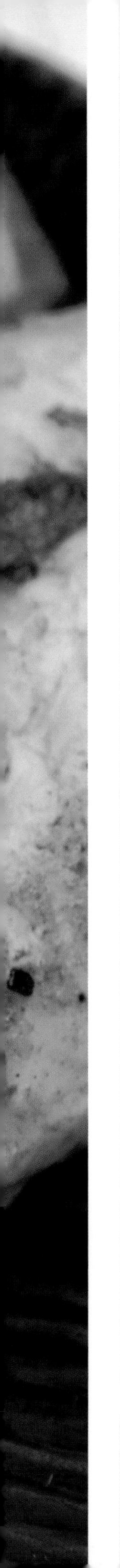

Grilled Catfish with Avocado Mayonnaise

6 fillets catfish

Marinade

2 tablespoons garlic, minced
2 teaspoons minced basil or cilantro
1 cup safflower oil

Avocado Mayonnaise

1 ripe avocado
1/2 teaspoon salt
1 tablespoon lime juice
1 teaspoon minced basil
1/2 teaspoon minced garlic
1 tablespoon herbal vinegar
1 teaspoon Dijon mustard
3 egg yolks
Remaining marinade (strain basil and garlic from oil, and cool oil in pan)

Marinade

1. *Mix marinade and soak fillets for 1 hour.*
2. *Remove fillets from marinade to hot greased grill.*
3. *Grill for 4-5 minutes each side, being careful not to overcook. Salt and pepper lightly.*
4. *Serve hot with avocado mayonnaise.*

Avocado Mayonnaise

1. *Puree avocado, salt and lime juice in food processor.*
2. *In saucepan, simmer basil and garlic in vinegar until almost completely evaporated.*
3. *Add remains of pan to blender with mustard and egg yolks.*
4. *Blend until smooth and, with motor running, add remaining oil from marinade. Blend until creamy and thick.*
5. *Add avocado mixture to blender, and blend.*
6. *Keep warm in top of double boiler.*

Serves: 6. Per serving: Calories 829, Fat 74.2 g, Saturated Fat 10.9 g, Cholesterol 594 mg, Sodium 306 mg, Carbohydrate 6.9 g, Fiber 3.8 g, Protein 33.2 g.

Rainbow Trout with Tarragon Cream Sauce

4 whole cleaned rainbow trout

Tarragon Cream Sauce

1/4 cup olive oil
1/4 cup whipping cream
1 tablespoon red wine vinegar
1 tablespoon parsley, finely chopped
1 egg yolk, beaten
1/2 teaspoon dried tarragon
1/4 teaspoon black pepper
1 small clove garlic, minced

Walnut Butter Sauce

1/2 cup walnuts
1/2 cup butter
3 tablespoons wine

1. *Grill rainbow trout on well-oiled grid or in well-oiled wire grill basket on covered grill, over medium-hot briquets 3-5 minutes, or until fish flakes easily when tested with fork. Turn once.*

2. *For Tarragon Cream Sauce, combine all ingredients in bowl. Beat with wire whip. Serve cool.*

3. *For Walnut Butter Sauce, sauté walnuts in 2 tablespoons butter. Reduce heat and add remaining butter. Stir until melted. Stir in wine. Serve warm.*

4. *Serve trout covered in Walnut Butter Sauce with Tarragon Cream Sauce for dipping.*

Per serving: Calories 307, Fat 24.8 g, Saturated Fat 6 g, Cholesterol 250 mg, Sodum 39 mg, Carbohydrate 1.7 g, Fiber 0 g, Protein 19.3 g.

Smoked Sausage Sandwiches

1 pound smoked sausage
1/4 cup orange juice
1 teaspoon dried oregano leaves
1 red onion, quartered
2 green bell peppers, seeded and cut into 1/2-inch-thick strips
3 pita bread rounds, cut in half
Green leaf lettuce
1/2 cup Colby cheese, shredded
1/2 cup Monterey Jack cheese, shredded
Brown spicy mustard to taste

1. *Preheat grill.*
2. *Diagonal-cut smoked sausage into thirty 1/2-inch-thick slices.*
3. *Combine orange juice and oregano in a small bowl. Stir well.*
4. *Separate layers of red onion quarters.*
5. *Place sausage, onion and bell peppers alternately on 6 metal skewers. Brush with orange juice mixture.*
6. *Place skewers on grill, and cook, covered, at moderate heat for 6-8 minutes, or until vegetables are tender, but crisp, and sausage is thoroughly heated. Turn skewers frequently, and baste with orange juice mixture.*
7. *Near the end of grilling time, set pita halves on the grill to warm.*
8. *Remove skewers and bread from grill. Line pita with lettuce. Slide kabob from skewers into pita pockets.*
9. *Sprinkle tops with cheese, and serve with brown spicy mustard.*

Serves: 6. Per serving: Calories 544, Fat 41.2 g, Saturated Fat 17.3 g, Cholesterol 81 mg, Sodium 851 mg, Carbohydrate 23.3 g, Fiber 2 g, Protein 20.3 g.

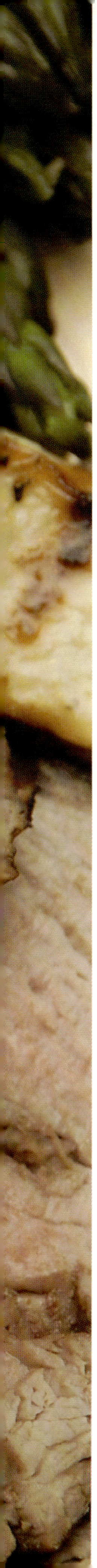

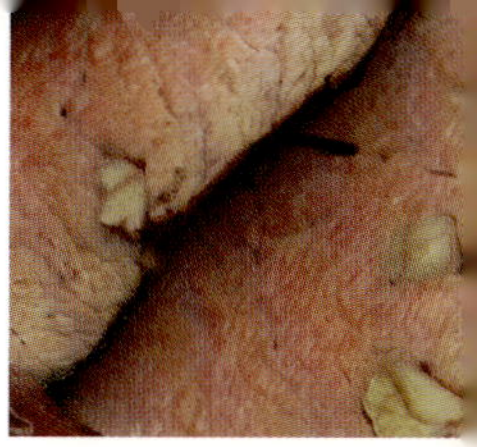

Tenderloin Rio Grande

10 cloves garlic, quartered
1 (4-pound) thick sirloin
4 tablespoons black pepper
1/2 bottle sauterne wine
5 tablespoons loose leaf basil
2 tablespoons stone ground mustard
1/2 cup olive oil
3 tablespoons salt

1. *Insert garlic quarters in beef tenderloin.*
2. *Mix together next 6 ingredients.*
3. *Place tenderloin in pan, and pour on marinade; marinate 1-2 hours.*
4. *Remove, grill 15 minutes each side, basting frequently with marinade.*
5. *Do not overcook. The meat will have a rare appearance because of the absorbed marinade.*
6. *To serve, crosscut on grain.*

Serves: 8. Per serving: Calories 791, Fat 67.7 g, Saturated Fat 23.4 g, Cholesterol 160 mg, Sodium 2763 mg, Carbohydrate 3.7 g, Fiber 0.9 g, Protein 41.6 g.

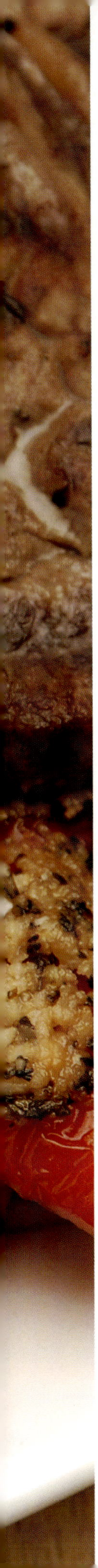

Steaks with Parmesan-Grilled Vegetables

2 Porterhouse steaks, cut 1-inch-thick
1 tablespoon garlic, minced
2 teaspoons dried basil
1 teaspoon black pepper
1/3 cup Parmesan cheese
2 tablespoons olive oil
2 tablespoons red wine vinegar
2 medium red bell peppers, quartered
1 large red onion, sliced 1/2-inch-thick

1. *Preheat grill to medium.*
2. *Combine garlic, basil and pepper. Remove 4 tablespoons; press into steaks.*
3. *Add cheese, oil and vinegar to remaining seasoning; mix well.*
4. *Place steaks in center of cooking grid; arrange vegetables around steaks.*
5. *Grill steaks, uncovered, turning occasionally, 14-16 minutes for medium rare to medium. Internal temperature is 150 to 160 degrees.*
6. *Grill bell peppers 12-15 minutes and onion 15-20 minutes, or until tender, turning once.*
7. *Brush vegetables with cheese mixture during last 10 minutes.*
8. *Carve steaks. Season with salt and pepper to taste. Serve with vegetables.*

Serves: 4. Per serving: Calories 396, Fat 17.7 g, Saturated Fat 5.4 g, Cholesterol 143 mg, Sodium 289 mg, Carbohydrate 6.3 g, Fiber 1.5 g, Protein 52.5 g.

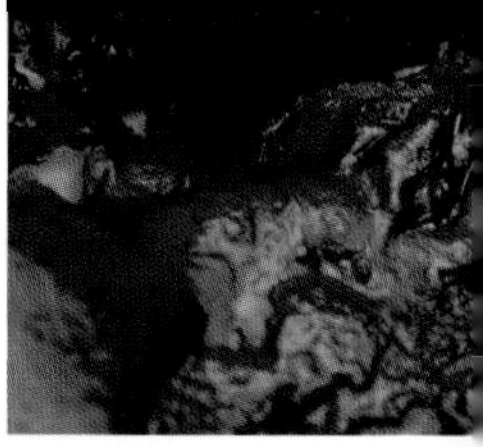

Tangy Southern Barbecued Ribs

1 bottle (18-ounce) barbecue sauce
1 teaspoon hot pepper sauce
1/2 teaspoon garlic powder
3 pounds pork spareribs or backribs

1. *Mix barbecue sauce, hot pepper sauce and garlic powder. Reserve 1/2 cup of this mixture, and set aside.*
2. *Place ribs, bone-side down, on greased grill over low coals.*
3. *Grill, uncovered, 30 minutes on each side. Brush with barbecue sauce mixture, and continue grilling 30 minutes, or until cooked through, turning and brushing with barbecue sauce mixture every 10 minutes.*
4. *Serve with reserved sauce mixture.*

Serves: 6. Per serving: Calories 470, Fat 35 g, Saturated Fat 13 g, Protein 26 g, Carbohydrate 11 g, Fiber 1 g, Cholesterol110 mg, Sodium 800 mg.

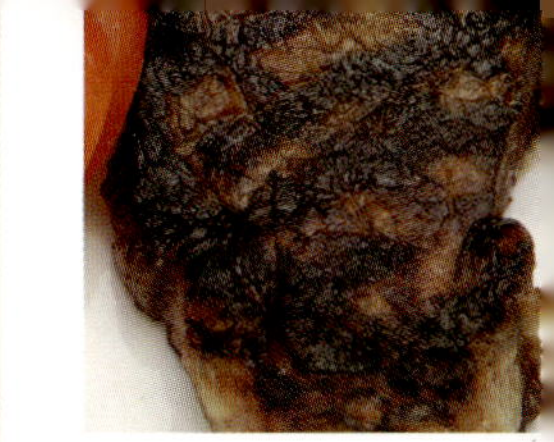

Marinated Blue Cheese Steak

3 teaspoons extra virgin olive oil, divided
2 teaspoons balsamic vinegar
2 cloves garlic, minced
Salt, to taste
Pepper, to taste
2 8-ounce New York strip steaks
1 1/4 cup sliced mushrooms
4 ounces blue cheese crumbles

1. *In a small bowl, whisk together two teaspoons of olive oil, balsamic vinegar, garlic, salt and pepper.*
2. *Place the steaks in a container just large enough to hold them. Pour the olive oil mixture over the steaks, and rub in well over both sides.*
3. *Allow the steak to marinate in the refrigerate for a minimum of 30 minutes, or up to two hours.*
4. *Grill steaks for 5 minutes per side, or until desired doneness is accomplished.*
5. *While steaks are grilling, sauté mushrooms with a pinch of salt over medium-high heat, stirring constantly for 5 minutes, or until mushrooms have given up most of their liquid. (If desired, season the mushrooms with fresh ground black pepper.)*
6. *Add the blue cheese crumbles, and stir to blend.*
7. *When the steaks are ready, smother with mushrooms and blue cheese.*

Serves: 2. Per serving: Calories 55, Fat 26 g, Saturated Fat 10 g, Fiber 1 g, Protein 9 g, Carbohydrate 9 g, Cholesterol 145 mg, Sodium 420 mg.

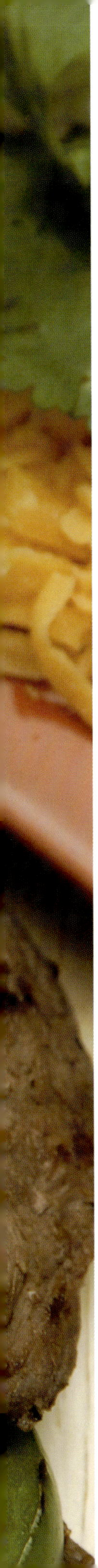

Branding Iron Fajitas

3 lb beef tenderloin, trimmed
1 teaspoon garlic powder
1 teaspoon cumin
1/2 teaspoon salt
1/2 teaspoon black pepper
1 (16-ounce bottle) Italian dressing (not creamy Italian)

12 flour tortillas
1 (8-ounce) jar picante sauce, hot or mild
2 cups grated cheese
1/2 cup chopped onion
2 cups shredded lettuce
1 cup sour cream
1 cup guacamole

1. *Cut meat across grain in strips 1-inch to 1 1/2-inches wide by 5 inches long.*
2. *Generously sprinkle all meat strips with garlic powder, cumin, salt and pepper.*
3. *Place meat strips in a plastic container with a tight fitting lid; cover with Italian dressing, thoroughly coating all pieces.*
4. *Cover container and refrigerate for a minimum of 12 hours.*
5. *Turn meat over in dressing 2 times during marination period.*
6. *Prepare coals to medium hot temperature.*
7. *Remove meat strips from dressing; drain and place on grill.*
8. *Cover grill and cook 10-12 minutes, turning 3 times during cooking.*
9. *Serve with flour tortillas, picante sauce, cheese, onion, lettuce and sour cream.*

Serves: 6. Per serving: Calories 1,352, Fat 102.7 g, Saturated Fat 35.1 g, Cholesterol 163 mg, Sodium 1,638 mg, Carbohydrate 56.8 g, Fiber 3 g, Protein 50.1 g.

Old San Antonio Fajitas

2 pounds top sirloin
Fajita seasoning
1 cup vegetable oil
1/4 cup salsa, mild or hot
2 cloves fresh garlic, smashed
2 limes, juiced
2 cups grated cheeese
6-8 flour tortillas, warmed
2 cups picante sauce
Guacamole

1. *Rub steak with fajita seasoning.*
2. *Combine oil, salsa, garlic and lime juice.*
3. *Marinate meat for 6-8 hours in the salsa mixture.*
4. *Cook over charcoal, or bake in oven, for 3 hours at 275 degrees.*
5. *Cut into strips, and serve in hot flour tortillas with cheese, picante sauce and guacamole.*

Serves: 6. Per serving: Calories 695, Fat 52.1 g, Saturated Fat 11.5 g, Cholesterol 112 mg, Sodium 1145 mg, Carbohydrate 173 g, Fiber 1.3 g, Protein 39.2 g.

Ozark Pork Steaks

6 large pork steaks

Ozark Sauce

3 cups barbecue sauce
1/2 cup clover honey
1/4 cup soy sauce
1/4 cup raspberry vinaigrette
1/4 cup parsley flakes
1/2 teaspoon ground cinnamon
1/2 teaspoon black pepper
1/8 teaspoon celery seed
1/8 teaspoon nutmeg, ground
1/4 cup peach juice

1. *Combine all sauce ingredients in a blender, and blend for 2 minutes.*
2. *Light charcoal briquets in grill.*
3. *Soak hickory chips in pan with water.*
4. *Add handful of chips to charcoal. Let fire and chips smoke about 15-20 minutes.*
5. *Baste the pork steaks with the sauce, and place on the back of the grill rack.*
6. *Smoke the pork steaks, turning every 45 minutes and basting with the sauce to keep steaks from drying out.*
7. *Smoke approximately 4-5 hours, adding a handful of chips every 45 minutes.*

Serves: 6. Per serving: Calories 447, Fat 15.7 g, Saturated Fat 3.8 g, Cholesterol 103 mg, Sodium 1541 mg, Carbohydrate 41.9 g, Fiber 2.1 g, Protein 34.4 g.

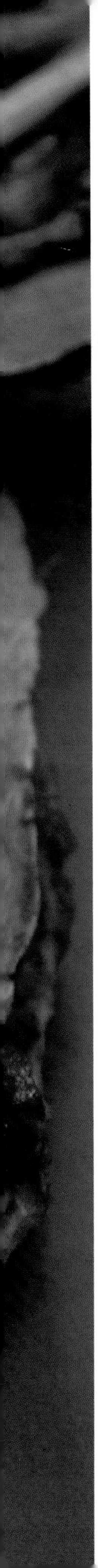

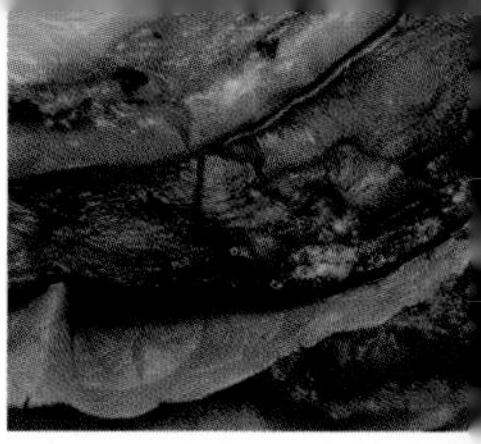

Portobello Burgers Italian Style

4 large Portobello mushrooms
1/4 cup olive oil
1/2 teaspoon dried basil
4 garlic cloves, crushed
Black pepper to taste
4 thick slices red or yellow onion
4 medium tomatoes, halved
4 whole wheat or sourdough sandwich rolls, split
Marinara sauce
4 slices Provolone cheese
8 leaves of Romaine lettuce

1. *Remove stems from mushrooms.*
2. *Mix oil, garlic, basil and pepper.*
3. *Brush mushroom caps, onion and tomato halves with oil, and grill on a piece of aluminum foil until tender, but not falling apart.*
4. *Cook over medium heat, about 4 minutes per side. Check for doneness by making a small slit in one cap. A satiny texture indicates it is done. Caps will also shrink and flatten as they cook.*
5. *Onions will caramelize, and tomatoes should be tender.*
6. *Remove vegetables from heat as they reach the right degree of doneness.*
7. *Set aside and cover to keep warm.*
8. *Spread each side of roll with 1 tablespoon of marinara sauce.*
9. *Layer vegetables on warm rolls with Provolone cheese and Romaine lettuce.*
10. *Serve immediately.*

Chef's tip: For a festive touch, use a toothpick to spear each burger with a black olive placed on top of a basil leaf sprig.

Serves: 4. Per serving: Calories 405, Fat 24.6 g, Protein 16.8 g, Carbohydrate 34.2 g, Fiber 10.6 g, Cholesterol 19.6 mg, Sodium 636.9 mg.

the GLORY of GRILLING

Grilling meats and vegetables over a wood fire has been around since the beginning of time. However, the development of charcoal as a primary source of heat for the outdoor grill came from the same inventive mind that introduced the revolutionary process of manufacturing automobiles on an assembly line.

Henry Ford realized that he was wasting a great deal of money on the enormous amount of wood necessary to build his Model A cars. There were piles of sawdust everywhere he looked. In an effort to transform his waste into a profit, Ford began making charcoal briquettes and selling them to steel mills, as well as to anyone else who needed a quick, inexpensive and efficient way to create heat and energy.

It wasn't long before people were hauling charcoal briquettes home and using them for outdoor cooking. The widespread use of briquettes persuaded someone to invent the charcoal grill. And outdoor cooking was never the same.

Of course, there is a long-standing debate on which is better – the charcoal grill or the gas grill.

Both have a definite place in your backyard. Charcoal grills are more versatile, and they cook hotter. You can burn wood in charcoal grills, and the various woods – hickory, mesquite, apple, etc.– provide your meats and vegetables with more flavor. It's easier to smoke in a charcoal grill. However, charcoal grills tend to be messier, and they gradually lose their heat and require you to restoke them every hour or so.

Gas grills, on the other hand, provide a constant and consistent heat with the twist of a knob. A propane tank can burn for as long as twenty hours. And gas grills offer such time-saving features as push button lighting. However, it's virtually impossible to get a rich, smoky flavor in gas grills. Unlike charcoal, gas doesn't add any taste at all.

Some people have solved the great debate this way. They use a gas grill during the week when they tend to be running short of time, then turn to a charcoal grill on the weekend when they have more leisure time available to master the fine art of outdoor cooking.